Goodman's Five-Star ACTIVITY BOOKS

Test-Taker Practice Series

LEVEL B

Burton Goodman

JAMESTOWN PUBLISHERS

a division of NTC/CONTEMPORARY PUBLISHING GROUP
Lincolnwood, Illinois USA

Acknowledgments

Stories, articles, adaptations, and other instructional materials by Burton Goodman.
The author wishes to express profound gratitude to Matthew Goodman for his invaluable assistance.

Cover Design
    Karen Christoffersen
Interior Illustrations
    Other Brother Design

ISBN: 0-8092-0446-0
Published by Jamestown Publishers,
a division of NTC/Contemporary Publishing Group, Inc.,
4255 West Touhy Avenue,
Lincolnwood (Chicago), Illinois, 60712-1975, U.S.A.
© 2001 by Burton Goodman
All rights reserved. No part of this book may be reproduced, stored in a retrieval system, or transmitted in any form or by any means, electronic, mechanical, photocopying, recording, or otherwise, without prior written permission of the publisher.
Manufactured in the United States of America.

6 7 8 9 10 11 12 118 09 08 07 06

CONTENTS

About the Series 4

Cookies from the Sky 6
a short story

Alex Haley's *Roots* 14
a true story

A Tall Story 22
a short story

Going for the Gold 32
a true story

Foods from Mexico 40
a true story

Li and the Rock 48
a short story

All About the Wolf 56
a true story

Test-Taker Score Chart   Inside back cover

ABOUT THE SERIES

Goodman's Five-Star Activity Books, Level B reinforces and extends the exercises and literary themes in *Adventures* and *More Adventures* in *Goodman's Five-Star Stories,* Level B. This activity book can be used in conjunction with *Adventures* and *More Adventures,* or it can be used on a completely independent basis.

Goodman's Five-Star Activity Books
Test-Taker Practice Series

The *Goodman's Five-Star Activity Books* series has been specially designed to help students master the kinds of exercises most frequently found on standardized tests. The series uses high-quality multicultural nonfiction and fiction materials to familiarize students with the kinds of questions they are likely to encounter. At the same time, the books offer students numerous opportunities to improve their language arts skills and their test scores through practice.

Each book in the series focuses on developing skills and competencies in reading comprehension, mechanics, and writing. Provision is also made for study skills practice.

The **Reading Skills** section provides students with 10 standardized questions with an emphasis on critical thinking and vocabulary. The **Mechanics** section offers repeated practice in capitalization, punctuation, the comma, spelling, and grammar. The **Writing** section requires students to respond to a wide variety of specific and open-ended writing tasks.

The series includes a practical Test-Taker self-scoring feature that enables students to score and record their results.

Used along with the books in *Goodman's Five-Star Stories*, or on an independent basis, I feel certain that the *Goodman's Five-Star Activity Books* will help students develop the confidence and competency to improve their test scores. In addition, the books will help readers master many of the essential language arts skills they need for success in school and in life.

Burton Goodman

DIRECTIONS
Read the story. Then answer the questions.

Cookies from the Sky

A woodcutter lived in a little house with his wife. He was not very smart. But his wife was very, very clever. He was always doing silly things. His wife always got him out of trouble.

One day the woodcutter was in a forest. He was cutting down trees. The woodcutter came to a tall tree. He saw a bag next to the tree. He opened the bag. It was filled with pieces of silver.

The woodcutter hurried home. He showed the bag of silver to his wife. "Look what I have found!" he said. "We are rich! We are rich!"

"Yes," said the woodcutter's wife. "But we must be careful. A robber must have lost this bag of silver. He might come back. We must find a very good place to hide the bag. There is an old tree in the garden. The tree has a hole in it. We can put the bag of silver there."

They went into the garden. They hid the bag in the tree. Then they went back to the house.

"Remember," said the wife. "Do not tell anyone about the silver. Do not say a word about it."

For additional exercises and a story with a similar plot, see "The Day It Snowed Tortillas" in *Adventures* in *Goodman's Five-Star Stories,* Level B.

"I will not say a word," the woodcutter replied.

But the wife knew her husband very well. She knew that he could not keep a secret. She was afraid that he would tell everyone about the bag of silver.

Later, she went back to the old tree. She took out the bag of silver. She hid it under a pile of hay.

That night the woodcutter fell asleep right away. The wife went to the kitchen. She began to bake. She made some cookies She put them into a basket. Then she went to sleep.

The next morning the woodcutter's wife got up very early. She went down to the river. The fishing boats were coming in. She bought some fish. She put them into the basket.

The woodcutter's wife walked into the woods. She put a few fish along the path. She put a few fish under a tree. She put a few fish near some flowers. The woodcutter's wife walked on. Then she took the cookies out of the basket. She threw the cookies into the air. Down they fell. They landed on the leaves. They landed on the rocks and on top of some bushes.

Then the wife went home. The woodcutter was just getting up. She said to him, "Let us go fishing today. We can fish in the woods. We can fish on the ground."

"We can fish on the ground in the woods?" the woodcutter asked.

"Yes," said the wife. "You will see. You will see."

They ate breakfast. Then they went into the woods. The woodcutter found a few fish along the path. He found a few fish under a tree. He found a few fish by some flowers.

"Look!" he cried out. "See how many fish I have caught! I like fishing in the woods!"

They walked on some more. The woodcutter saw cookies everywhere. He was surprised. Cookies were on the leaves. Cookies were on the rocks. Cookies were on top of the bushes.

"Look at all of these cookies!" the woodcutter said.

"Yes," said his wife. "It rained cookies last night."

"You are right!" the woodcutter said. "It rained cookies last night."

A few days later a man came to the house. The wife knew at once that he was the robber.

The man said, "Your husband has been talking to people in town. He said that he found a bag filled with silver."

The wife began to laugh. "Oh," she said. "He is always saying silly things. He likes to say that we have lots of silver."

The woodcutter said, "But it *is* so! I did find a bag of silver. We hid the bag in a tree outside."

"When was that?" the robber asked.

The woodcutter said, "It was the day we went fishing in the woods. I caught some fish along the path and under a tree. I caught some fish by the flowers."

The robber stared at the man. "Are you sure of that?" the robber asked.

"Oh, yes," the woodcutter said. "I remember that day very well. It rained cookies the night before."

The robber got angry. "You caught fish on the ground! It rained cookies! You must be a fool! Show me the tree!"

They went and looked in the tree. Of course, nothing was there. The robber got on his horse and rode away. He kept saying, "It rained cookies! I never heard of such a thing!"

The robber never came back. So the woodcutter and his wife lived a *very* good life.

I. Reading Skills

Fill in the circle next to the right answer.

1. This story is mostly about
   - Ⓐ a robber.
   - Ⓑ how to catch fish in the woods.
   - Ⓒ the kind of work a woodcutter does.
   - Ⓓ how a woodcutter's wife tricked a robber.

2. Which words belong in Box 1?
   - Ⓐ did not like the woodcutter
   - Ⓑ knew the woodcutter very well
   - Ⓒ was sorry the woodcutter found the bag of silver
   - Ⓓ went fishing every day

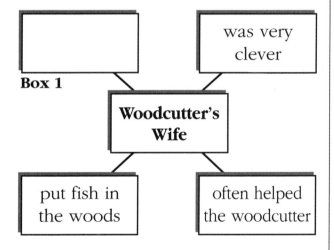

3. The wife hid the bag of silver
   - Ⓐ under a pile of hay.
   - Ⓑ in a hole in the ground.
   - Ⓒ behind a big rock.
   - Ⓓ under the bed.

4. Why did the wife take the bag of silver out of the old tree?
   - Ⓐ to keep it all for herself
   - Ⓑ to hide it from some children
   - Ⓒ to hide it from the robber
   - Ⓓ to surprise the woodcutter

5. Which sentence is true?
   - Ⓐ The woodcutter thought that it rained cookies from the sky.
   - Ⓑ The wife thought that it rained cookies from the sky.
   - Ⓒ The robber thought that it rained cookies from the sky.
   - Ⓓ It rained cookies from the sky.

Answers

1. Ⓐ Ⓑ Ⓒ Ⓓ
2. Ⓐ Ⓑ Ⓒ Ⓓ
3. Ⓐ Ⓑ Ⓒ Ⓓ
4. Ⓐ Ⓑ Ⓒ Ⓓ
5. Ⓐ Ⓑ Ⓒ Ⓓ

Go on ▶

6. Why did the robber think that the woodcutter was a fool?
   - Ⓐ The woodcutter said that he was a fool.
   - Ⓑ Everyone in town said that the woodcutter was a fool.
   - Ⓒ The robber knew the woodcutter very well.
   - Ⓓ The woodcutter said things that sounded very silly.

7. At the end of the story, the wife probably felt
   - Ⓐ sad.
   - Ⓑ pleased.
   - Ⓒ angry.
   - Ⓓ frightened.

8. The woodcutter was working in a forest. The word *forest* means
   - Ⓐ land covered with trees.
   - Ⓑ a small garden.
   - Ⓒ a park.
   - Ⓓ a street.

9. "I will not say a word," the woodcutter replied. The word *replied* means
   - Ⓐ thought.
   - Ⓑ wished.
   - Ⓒ answered.
   - Ⓓ tried.

10. The woodcutter could not keep a secret. What is a *secret*?
    - Ⓐ a good job
    - Ⓑ a lot of money
    - Ⓒ something that everyone knows
    - Ⓓ something you don't want other people to know

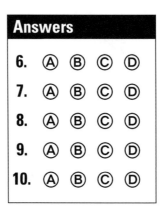

Answers
6. Ⓐ Ⓑ Ⓒ Ⓓ
7. Ⓐ Ⓑ Ⓒ Ⓓ
8. Ⓐ Ⓑ Ⓒ Ⓓ
9. Ⓐ Ⓑ Ⓒ Ⓓ
10. Ⓐ Ⓑ Ⓒ Ⓓ

How many questions did you get right? Circle your score below. Then fill in your **Reading Skills** score on the **Test-Taker Score Chart** on the inside of the back cover.

Number Correct	1	2	3	4	5	6	7	8	9	10
My Score	10	20	30	40	50	60	70	80	90	100

Go on ▶

II. Mechanics (capital letters, punctuation, commas, spelling, and grammar)

Fill in the circle next to the right answer.

1. Which sentence needs a capital letter?
   - Ⓐ We read this story on Friday.
   - Ⓑ it is about a woodcutter and his wife.
   - Ⓒ The robber rode out of town on his horse.

2. Which sentence has a mistake in punctuation?
   - Ⓐ The woodcutter found a bag of silver.
   - Ⓑ His wife was afraid that the robber would come back
   - Ⓒ Did the robber come back?

3. Which sentence needs a comma?
   - Ⓐ They walked by trees, plants, and flowers.
   - Ⓑ The basket was filled with cookies and fish.
   - Ⓒ The cookies landed on rocks bushes, and leaves.

4. Which sentence has a word that is spelled wrong? Look at the **underlined** words.
   - Ⓐ The woodcutter's wife began makeing some cookies.
   - Ⓑ She began taking them out of the basket.
   - Ⓒ The fishing boats were coming in.

5. Which sentence has a mistake in grammar?
   - Ⓐ The woodcutter and his wife was happy together.
   - Ⓑ She did many smart things.
   - Ⓒ They were able to live a very good life.

Answers
1. Ⓐ Ⓑ Ⓒ Ⓓ
2. Ⓐ Ⓑ Ⓒ Ⓓ
3. Ⓐ Ⓑ Ⓒ Ⓓ
4. Ⓐ Ⓑ Ⓒ Ⓓ
5. Ⓐ Ⓑ Ⓒ Ⓓ

How many questions did you get right? Circle your score below. Then fill in your **Mechanics** score on the **Test-Taker Score Chart** on the inside of the back cover.

Number Correct	1	2	3	4	5
Your Score	20	40	60	80	100

Go on ▶

III. Writing

Answer the questions. You may look back at the story as often as you wish.

1. In "Cookies from the Sky," the woodcutter's wife did many things. In the box below, list five things she did. One has already been listed for you.

    Things the Woodcutter's Wife Did

    1. She took the bag of silver out of the tree.

    2.

    3.

    4.

    5.

2. Look at the list above. Circle two things on the list. Then tell why the woodcutter's wife did those things.

    _____
    _____
    _____
    _____
    _____

3. The woodcutter was lucky to have a very clever wife. Explain why.

_____
_____
_____
_____
_____
_____
_____
_____

4. Suppose that the robber had found the bag of silver in the old tree. Tell how you think the story would have ended.

_____
_____
_____
_____
_____
_____
_____
_____

DIRECTIONS
Read this true story. Then answer the questions.

Alex Haley's Roots

Alex Haley is a very important writer. His book *Roots* came out in 1976. It sold more than 500,000 copies.

Roots tells the story of Alex Haley's family. The book goes back in time about 200 years. It goes all the way back to a man named Kunta Kinte.

Kunta Kinte lived in West Africa. He was taken from his home and sold as a slave.[1] That is how Haley's family came to the United States from Africa.

Haley wanted to write a book about his family. He first thought about writing the book when he was a boy. At the time Haley lived in Tennessee.

Haley often talked to his grandmother. They sat on the porch. She told him stories about their family.

Haley's grandmother told him about her own great-grandfather. She said that his last name was Kinte. She told Alex many stories.

Haley was always sorry when the stories ended. He

1. **slave:** someone who is owned by another person. A slave is forced to work for that person.

For additional exercises and more stories from West Africa, see "Anansi and the Sea" in *Adventures* and "The Man Who Said Moo" in *More Adventures* in *Goodman's Five-Star Stories*, Level B.

told himself that one day he would write a book. It would tell about the people in his family. He wanted other people to know how hard his family's lives had been.

Later Haley became a writer. He wrote stories. Then he felt that he was ready. He was going to write the book about his family.

Haley decided to go to West Africa. He flew to a country called The Gambia. He had heard about an old man who lived there. People said that the man was very wise. They said that he knew all about the Kinte family.

The old man lived in a little village. The trip to the village was long and hard. Haley had to take a boat down the Gambia River. Finally, Haley found the old man.

Haley listened to the old man's stories for two hours. Haley did not ask any questions. He just listened.

Then the old man told a story about Kunta Kinte. He had been taken away as a slave. The old man said that Kunta Kinte "went away from the village to chop wood." The old man finished the story by saying that "he was never seen again."

Haley could not believe his ears. He was filled with joy. Kunta Kinte was the man his grandmother had told him about! Haley had found what he was looking for!

Now Haley knew that he could tell his family's story. First, he had to learn as much as he could about his family. Haley did that for the next 12 years. He talked to more than 1,000 people. He visited many libraries around the world.

One day Haley said to himself, "I wonder what Kunta Kinte's trip to the United States was like. I must find out."

Haley went back to West Africa. He found a ship that was sailing to the United States. The ship was not carrying passengers. It was carrying cargo.[2] But Haley paid to ride on that ship.

2. cargo: things that are carried by a ship to be sold in different places.

It took 10 days for the ship to reach the United States. Each night Haley went to the place where the cargo was kept. It was cold and dark there. Haley lay down on a wooden board. He slept there all night. That was what Kunta Kinte had done. Haley tried to imagine how Kunta Kinte had felt. Haley tried to imagine what Kunta Kinte had thought about during the trip.

Haley wrote about Kunta Kinte's trip in *Roots*. Haley wrote down all of his family's stories. The book came out in September 1976. It was almost 700 pages long. People loved Haley's book. Everywhere, people talked about *Roots*.

The next year *Roots* was made into a movie for TV. The movie was 12 hours long. It took six nights to show the movie. People all across the country watched *Roots*. On the last night more than 90 million Americans watched it.

The book won many prizes. In 1977 it won a Pulitzer Prize. That meant that *Roots* was a very great book.

Alex Haley's trip was over. It had lasted for 12 years. It had taken Haley to Africa. Then it took him back home again. Haley had done what he had set out to do. He had loved his family's stories. Now the whole world knew them.

I. Reading Skills

Fill in the circle next to the right answer.

1. This story is mostly about
   - Ⓐ how Alex Haley wrote *Roots*.
   - Ⓑ life in West Africa.
   - Ⓒ an old man who lived in The Gambia.
   - Ⓓ a TV movie that many Americans watched.

2. Which words belong in Box 1?
   - Ⓐ did not write any stories
   - Ⓑ wrote *Roots* in 1996
   - Ⓒ loved his grandmother's stories
   - Ⓓ did not like his grandmother's stories

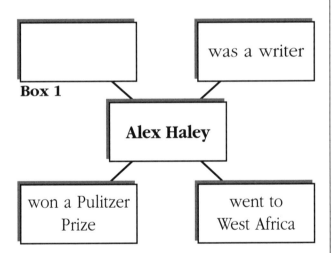

3. How long did it take Alex Haley to write *Roots*?
   - Ⓐ a year
   - Ⓑ 5 years
   - Ⓒ nearly 10 years
   - Ⓓ 12 years

4. When the old man told Haley about Kunta Kinte, Haley
   - Ⓐ felt very sad.
   - Ⓑ was very happy.
   - Ⓒ was not surprised.
   - Ⓓ did not believe what the old man said.

5. Haley went by ship from West Africa to the United States because he
   - Ⓐ loved to sail on ships.
   - Ⓑ was afraid to fly on a plane.
   - Ⓒ wanted to see what Kunta Kinte's trip had been like.
   - Ⓓ had friends who were on the ship.

Answers

1. Ⓐ Ⓑ Ⓒ Ⓓ
2. Ⓐ Ⓑ Ⓒ Ⓓ
3. Ⓐ Ⓑ Ⓒ Ⓓ
4. Ⓐ Ⓑ Ⓒ Ⓓ
5. Ⓐ Ⓑ Ⓒ Ⓓ

Go on ➤

6. Which sentence is true?
   - Ⓐ *Roots* is nearly 500 pages long.
   - Ⓑ *Roots* tells the story of Haley's family.
   - Ⓒ Fewer than 100,000 people read *Roots*.
   - Ⓓ *Roots* was not made into a TV show.

7. People probably liked reading *Roots* because
   - Ⓐ it was a very short book.
   - Ⓑ most readers knew many of the stories that Haley told.
   - Ⓒ people learned many interesting things.
   - Ⓓ all the stories in *Roots* were very funny.

8. After a long, hard trip, Haley finally got to the village. The word *finally* means
   - Ⓐ at last.
   - Ⓑ never.
   - Ⓒ almost.
   - Ⓓ quickly

9. Haley was the only passenger on the ship. What is a *passenger*?
   - Ⓐ a writer
   - Ⓑ a teacher
   - Ⓒ someone who goes to a place by bus, plane, train, or ship
   - Ⓓ someone who is afraid of the sea

10. Haley tried to imagine what had happened many years before. When you *imagine* something, you
    - Ⓐ like it.
    - Ⓑ write about it.
    - Ⓒ forget it.
    - Ⓓ try to think about what it was like.

Answers

6. Ⓐ Ⓑ Ⓒ Ⓓ
7. Ⓐ Ⓑ Ⓒ Ⓓ
8. Ⓐ Ⓑ Ⓒ Ⓓ
9. Ⓐ Ⓑ Ⓒ Ⓓ
10. Ⓐ Ⓑ Ⓒ Ⓓ

How many questions did you get right? Circle your score below. Then fill in your **Reading Skills** score on the **Test-Taker Score Chart** on the inside of the back cover.

Number Correct	1	2	3	4	5	6	7	8	9	10
My Score	10	20	30	40	50	60	70	80	90	100

Go on ▶

Alex Haley's *Roots*

II. Mechanics (capital letters, punctuation, commas, spelling, and grammar)

Fill in the circle next to the right answer.

1. Which sentence needs a capital letter?
   - Ⓐ Alex Haley went to africa.
   - Ⓑ Then he took a ship to the United States.
   - Ⓒ He visited libraries all over the world.

2. Which sentence has a mistake in punctuation?
   - Ⓐ Why was Haley so pleased.
   - Ⓑ He found a man who knew about Kunte Kinte.
   - Ⓒ That was great!

3. Which sentence needs a comma?
   - Ⓐ *Roots* is about Alex Haley's family.
   - Ⓑ More than 500,000 books were sold by December 1 1976.
   - Ⓒ The book was later made into a TV movie.

4. Which sentence has a word that is spelled wrong? Look at the **underlined** words.
   - Ⓐ Alex Haley never <u>stopped</u> trying to find out about his family.
   - Ⓑ After he wrote *Roots*, Haley kept <u>getting</u> prizes.
   - Ⓒ Alex and his grandmother were <u>siting</u> on the porch.

5. Which sentence has a mistake in grammar?
   - Ⓐ Alex Haley is a very important writer.
   - Ⓑ People all over the world have read his books.
   - Ⓒ Many people has also seen *Roots* on TV.

Answers

1. Ⓐ Ⓑ Ⓒ Ⓓ
2. Ⓐ Ⓑ Ⓒ Ⓓ
3. Ⓐ Ⓑ Ⓒ Ⓓ
4. Ⓐ Ⓑ Ⓒ Ⓓ
5. Ⓐ Ⓑ Ⓒ Ⓓ

How many questions did you get right? Circle your score below. Then fill in your **Mechanics** score on the **Test-Taker Score Chart** on the inside of the back cover.

Number Correct	1	2	3	4	5
Your Score	20	40	60	80	100

Go on ▶

III. Writing

Answer the questions. You may look back at the story as often as you wish.

1. In the box below, list some things that Alex Haley did to find out about his family.

Things Haley Did to Find Out about His Family

2. The book *Roots* "goes back in time about 200 years." Why didn't Haley go back just 50 or 100 years? Explain.

_____
_____
_____
_____
_____
_____

3. Write about an interesting person in your family. If you wish, write about a friend or someone you know. Be sure to tell the following:
   - who the person is
   - what the person looks like
   - why you picked that person

An Interesting Person

_____

_____

_____

_____

_____

_____

_____

_____

_____

_____

_____

_____

_____

_____

_____

DIRECTIONS
Read the story. Then answer the questions.

A Tall Story

Kumar Persaud was very tall. He was the tallest boy in his class. Kumar was very friendly with all of the children. But he never played with Steven, who lived in the house next to his.

One day Kumar's mother, Mrs. Persaud, spoke to him. She said, "Kumar, why don't you ever play with Steven?"

Kumar said. "Steven is very short. He is too short to be my friend."

Mrs. Persaud said, "Let me tell you a story." This is the story she told:

A lion had been out hunting all morning. He was hot and tired, so he lay down in the shade of a tree. He soon fell asleep.

A mouse happened to be walking by. He had never been so close to a lion. The mouse was curious. He went quietly up to the lion and looked at it.

"What an amazing beast!" said the mouse. "I must take a closer look." The next thing the mouse knew, he was walking up and down on top of the lion.

For additional exercises and a theme-related story, see "A River Story" in *More Adventures* in *Goodman's Five-Star Stories,* Level B.

The lion suddenly woke up. He threw his big paw over the mouse and held him tightly.

"What have I here?" roared the lion. "Why, I have a mouse! Well, a mouse is not much of a meal. But it is better than nothing at all."

The lion opened his great mouth to eat the mouse.

"Please, don't eat me!" begged the mouse. "Please let me go. If you do, I will never forget it. The time may come when I can help you."

The lion smiled. "Help me?" he said. "How could a little fellow like you help someone like me?"

The lion laughed. He laughed louder and louder. The idea seemed so silly! By now he was feeling happy. He lifted his paw, and the mouse scampered away.

Many months went by. One day the lion was walking in the woods. He came to a lake. He started to take a drink of water. Just then the lion smelled something. The lion knew that smell! It meant that people were near!

Suddenly the lion heard voices. "Get him! Get that lion!" called the voices.

The lion turned to run, but it was too late. He felt a strong rope around his neck and another around his body.

"Tie the lion to a tree!" a hunter cried out. "We can kill the lion later!"

They dragged the lion across the ground. They tied the lion to a tree. Then the hunters went on their way.

The lion roared. His roar was very loud. The mouse was passing by. He said, "That sounds like my friend, the lion."

The mouse soon came upon the lion. Two strong ropes held the lion to a tree.

"Well, well, well," the mouse said to the lion. "You seem to be in trouble."

The lion looked at the mouse. He wondered if the mouse was making fun of him.

Then the mouse said, "Don't you remember me? You once trapped me with your paw. But then you let me go."

"Oh, yes," said the lion. "Now I remember."

The mouse went on. "I said that I might help you one day." With that, the mouse put his sharp teeth against one rope. He gnawed and gnawed until he cut through it. Then he hopped to the other rope and gnawed right through it.

The lion was free!

"Thank you, friend, for saving my life," called the lion as he hurried away.

Mrs. Persaud turned to her son. She said, "Tell me, Kumar. What does this story teach?"

Kumar smiled and said, "It shows that a friend may be small—but a small friend can do great things."

I. Reading Skills

Fill in the circle next to the right answer.

1. This story is mostly about
   - Ⓐ Kumar Persaud and his friends.
   - Ⓑ some hunters.
   - Ⓒ why and how a mouse saved a lion.
   - Ⓓ the life of Mrs. Persaud.

2. Why didn't Kumar play with Steven?
   - Ⓐ Steven lived far away.
   - Ⓑ Steven was not friendly.
   - Ⓒ Steven was much older than Kumar.
   - Ⓓ Steven was much shorter than Kumar.

3. The lion let the mouse go because the lion
   - Ⓐ was afraid of the mouse.
   - Ⓑ started to laugh and felt happy.
   - Ⓒ knew that the mouse would help him one day.
   - Ⓓ had just finished eating lunch.

4. When the lion smelled the people, he probably
   - Ⓐ got frightened.
   - Ⓑ wondered who they were.
   - Ⓒ wondered how they got there.
   - Ⓓ was glad they came.

5. At the end of the story, the mouse knew that the lion was near because the mouse
   - Ⓐ smelled the lion.
   - Ⓑ saw the lion on top of a hill.
   - Ⓒ heard the lion roar.
   - Ⓓ followed the hunters.

6. Which sentence is *not* true?
   - Ⓐ The lion fell asleep because it was tired from hunting.
   - Ⓑ The hunters would have let the lion go.
   - Ⓒ At first, the lion was going to eat the mouse.
   - Ⓓ The mouse used his teeth to cut the ropes.

Answers

1. Ⓐ Ⓑ Ⓒ Ⓓ
2. Ⓐ Ⓑ Ⓒ Ⓓ
3. Ⓐ Ⓑ Ⓒ Ⓓ
4. Ⓐ Ⓑ Ⓒ Ⓓ
5. Ⓐ Ⓑ Ⓒ Ⓓ
6. Ⓐ Ⓑ Ⓒ Ⓓ

Go on ▶

7. The last sentence of "A Tall Story" shows that Kumar
   Ⓐ did not understand the story his mother told him.
   Ⓑ learned something important from the story.
   Ⓒ did not care about having friends.
   Ⓓ wished that he were not so tall.

8. The mouse went closer to the lion because the mouse was curious. When you are *curious,* you
   Ⓐ are brave.
   Ⓑ are silly.
   Ⓒ are small.
   Ⓓ want to know something.

9. "What an amazing beast!" said the mouse when he saw the lion. The word *amazing* means
   Ⓐ very surprising.
   Ⓑ quiet.
   Ⓒ hungry.
   Ⓓ sleepy.

10. The lion lifted its paw, and the mouse scampered away. The word *scampered* means
    Ⓐ ran quickly.
    Ⓑ moved slowly.
    Ⓒ began hopping.
    Ⓓ cried softly.

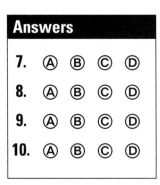

Answers
7. Ⓐ Ⓑ Ⓒ Ⓓ
8. Ⓐ Ⓑ Ⓒ Ⓓ
9. Ⓐ Ⓑ Ⓒ Ⓓ
10. Ⓐ Ⓑ Ⓒ Ⓓ

How many questions did you get right? Circle your score below. Then fill in your **Reading Skills** score on the **Test-Taker Score Chart** on the inside of the back cover.

Number Correct	1	2	3	4	5	6	7	8	9	10
My Score	10	20	30	40	50	60	70	80	90	100

Go on ▶

II. Mechanics (capital letters, punctuation, commas, spelling, and grammar)

Fill in the circle next to the right answer.

1. Which sentence needs a capital letter?
   - Ⓐ I read the story on a monday in October.
   - Ⓑ I remember that it was Columbus Day.
   - Ⓒ The mouse said, "Maybe I can help you some time."

2. Which sentence has a mistake in punctuation?
   - Ⓐ The mouse walked on top of the lion's body.
   - Ⓑ The lion opened its mouth to eat the mouse.
   - Ⓒ The lion needed the mouses help.

3. Which sentence needs a comma or commas?
   - Ⓐ Kumar, a tall boy, did not play with Steven.
   - Ⓑ Mrs. Persaud Kumar's mother told Kumar a story.
   - Ⓒ The lion, a large animal, was caught by the hunters.

4. Which sentence has a word that is spelled wrong? Look at the **underlined** words.
   - Ⓐ Kumar thought that Steven was to short to be his friend.
   - Ⓑ The hunters threw strong ropes around the lion.
   - Ⓒ Did the hunters surprise the lion?

5. Which sentence has a mistake in grammar?
   - Ⓐ Steven and Kumar are in the same class.
   - Ⓑ The mouse seen that the lion was in trouble.
   - Ⓒ The mouse quickly began to cut the ropes.

Answers

1. Ⓐ Ⓑ Ⓒ Ⓓ
2. Ⓐ Ⓑ Ⓒ Ⓓ
3. Ⓐ Ⓑ Ⓒ Ⓓ
4. Ⓐ Ⓑ Ⓒ Ⓓ
5. Ⓐ Ⓑ Ⓒ Ⓓ

How many questions did you get right? Circle your score below. Then fill in your **Mechanics** score on the **Test-Taker Score Chart** on the inside of the back cover.

Number Correct	1	2	3	4	5
Your Score	20	40	60	80	100

Go on ▶

III. Writing

Answer the questions. You may look back at the story as often as you wish.

1. At the beginning of the story, the lion laughed at the mouse. Explain why.

   _____
   _____
   _____
   _____

2. Why do you think Mrs. Persaud told Kumar the story of the mouse and the lion?

   I think that Mrs. Persaud told Kumar the story of the mouse and the lion because _____
   _____
   _____
   _____

3. Do you think that Kumar will be friendlier to Steven now? Explain why.

   _____
   _____
   _____
   _____

Go on ▶

4. What lessons does "A Tall Story" teach? List some in the box.

Some Lessons the Story Teaches

5. Write about a time when you helped a friend, or a friend helped you. Tell the time and the place, and explain what happened.

_____
_____
_____
_____
_____
_____
_____
_____
_____

IV. Study Skills

Reading a chart. "A Tall Story" tells about a lion and a mouse. The lion is one animal in the cat family. Of course, there are many other kinds of cats. Read the chart below. Then answer the questions.

	Some Cats in the Cat Family			
	Cat	**Where Cat Lives**	**Color of Cat**	**Interesting Cat Facts**
	Lion	Africa	yellow	The lion lives and hunts in groups.
	Tiger	India	yellow with black stripes	The tiger is the biggest and strongest of all cats.
	Bobcat	North America	yellow with black spots	The bobcat has a very short tail.
	Puma	North America and South America	gray in North America; brown in South America	The puma can jump 40 feet.
	House cat	all over the world	many colors	House cats have been pets for more than 4,000 years.

Go on ➤

1. How many kinds of cats are listed on the chart?

   _____

2. Where does the lion live?

   _____

3. Which cat is found all over the world?

   _____

4. What cat is yellow with black stripes?

   _____

5. Where does the puma live?

   _____

6. Which animal is the biggest and strongest of all of the cats?

   _____

7. What cat is most likely to be a pet?

   _____

8. Which cat has a very short tail?

   _____

9. What cat might be white, gray, black, or orange?

   _____

10. Which cat can jump 40 feet?

    _____

DIRECTIONS
Read this true story. Then answer the questions.

Going for the Gold

Gold! Some people like to wear gold. Other people like to save gold. Olympic runners try to finish first. They "go for the gold." The runner who wins the race gets a medal. It is made of gold.

People have always loved gold. But do you know what gold is? Do you know why people want it so much? Here are some facts about gold.

Gold is a metal. Like most metals, gold is usually found in the ground. If you have seen something made of gold, you know that gold is bright yellow.

Gold is very heavy. It is also very soft. Because it is soft, many things can be made of gold. A very small piece of gold can make a thin chain more than 50 feet long.

Gold is soft, but it is also very strong. Air does not harm it. The sun does not harm it. Saltwater does not harm it. Gold also lasts for a very long time. A gold ring made 1,000 years ago looks the same today.

People have always liked gold. About 5,000 years ago, the Egyptians made rings, pins, and necklaces of gold.

For additional exercises and more stories about gold, see "King Midas and the Golden Touch" in *Adventures* and "Hercules and the Three Golden Apples" in *More Adventures* in *Goodman's Five-Star Stories,* Level B.

Egyptian kings were buried with gold. Very old paintings on walls show Egyptians working with gold.

Long ago, the Greeks made cups and bowls of gold. Some of the cups and bowls are 3,000 years old. They still look beautiful today.

Gold was first used as money in China. The gold was cut into very small pieces. People used the gold pieces to buy things. That was about 3,000 years ago. About 500 years later, the first gold coins were made.

Long ago, countries in Europe started wars to get gold. There have been terrible fights over gold.

Of course, there are many stories about gold. In some stories kings try to get gold from their people. In other stories people try to steal gold. In still other stories people set out to find gold.

People have always looked for gold. Since the 1800s people have searched for gold in North America. Some gold was found in North Carolina in 1804. Later, some gold was found in a few other states in the South.

Much more gold was discovered in the West. In 1848 gold was discovered on John Sutter's land. He lived near Sacramento, California. Soon everyone had heard about Sutter and the gold. People wanted to get rich. They rushed to California from all over the country. That was known as the gold rush.

People also came from around the world. They came from as far away as China and Australia. More than 100,000 people moved to California during the gold rush.

These people thought that they would find gold. They all thought they would get rich. The truth is that very few people got rich. Most did not find any gold at all.

Going for the Gold 33

Life was very hard for these people. They lived in crowded towns and camps. They did not have enough food or water. Many people got sick. Many people died. After a while, people returned to their homes. They ended up as poor as they were when they went to California.

Today, most gold is found deep in the ground. The gold is dug up in mines. There are very big gold mines in South Africa and Russia. There are gold mines in the United States too.

Gold is brought up from these mines every day. That is good because people use more gold today than ever before. Gold is used for many more things than just coins and rings.

Gold is used in TV sets. It is used in the engines of airplanes and cars. It is even used to fill holes in teeth.

Gold is beautiful and strong. It is useful too. When people want you to know that something is *very, very* special, they may say that it is "as good as gold." Now that you know some facts about gold, you know just what that saying means!

I. Reading Skills

Fill in the circle next to the right answer.

1. This story is mostly about
   - Ⓐ what gold is and why it is important.
   - Ⓑ the early Egyptians.
   - Ⓒ countries that have gold mines.
   - Ⓓ John Sutter and the gold found on his land.

2. Which words belong in Box 1?
   - Ⓐ has very few uses
   - Ⓑ is not strong
   - Ⓒ lasts for a long time
   - Ⓓ can be harmed by the sun

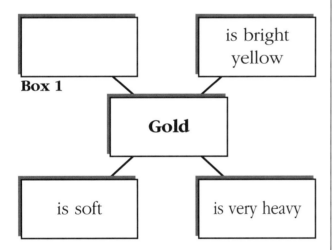

3. Which sentence is *not* true?
   - Ⓐ Long ago, the Greeks made cups and bowls of gold.
   - Ⓑ Salt water can harm gold.
   - Ⓒ The air does not harm gold.
   - Ⓓ Today, most gold is dug up in mines.

4. When Olympic runners "go for the gold," they
   - Ⓐ try to buy gold.
   - Ⓑ hurry to places where gold is found.
   - Ⓒ try to finish first.
   - Ⓓ wear chains made of gold.

5. Gold was first used as money in
   - Ⓐ the United States.
   - Ⓑ South Africa.
   - Ⓒ Russia.
   - Ⓓ China.

Answers

1. Ⓐ Ⓑ Ⓒ Ⓓ
2. Ⓐ Ⓑ Ⓒ Ⓓ
3. Ⓐ Ⓑ Ⓒ Ⓓ
4. Ⓐ Ⓑ Ⓒ Ⓓ
5. Ⓐ Ⓑ Ⓒ Ⓓ

Go on ▶

6. What happened to most of the people who went to California during the gold rush?
   - Ⓐ They returned home poor.
   - Ⓑ They found gold.
   - Ⓒ They became rich.
   - Ⓓ They were happy with their new lives.

7. The story says that gold
   - Ⓐ is not a metal.
   - Ⓑ was found all over the South.
   - Ⓒ is never found deep in the ground.
   - Ⓓ is both beautiful and useful.

8. Egyptian kings were buried with gold. The word *buried* means
   - Ⓐ dressed in.
   - Ⓑ given.
   - Ⓒ told about.
   - Ⓓ put in the earth.

9. There have been terrible battles over gold. The word *battles* means
   - Ⓐ fights.
   - Ⓑ stories.
   - Ⓒ dreams.
   - Ⓓ trips.

10. Gold was discovered in California in 1848. The word *discovered* means
    - Ⓐ lost.
    - Ⓑ found.
    - Ⓒ bought.
    - Ⓓ sold.

Answers

6. Ⓐ Ⓑ Ⓒ Ⓓ
7. Ⓐ Ⓑ Ⓒ Ⓓ
8. Ⓐ Ⓑ Ⓒ Ⓓ
9. Ⓐ Ⓑ Ⓒ Ⓓ
10. Ⓐ Ⓑ Ⓒ Ⓓ

How many questions did you get right? Circle your score below. Then fill in your **Reading Skills** score on the **Test-Taker Score Chart** on the inside of the back cover.

Number Correct	1	2	3	4	5	6	7	8	9	10
My Score	10	20	30	40	50	60	70	80	90	100

Go on ▶

II. Mechanics (capital letters, punctuation, commas, spelling, and grammar)

Fill in the circle next to the right answer.

1. Which sentence needs a capital letter?
   - Ⓐ More gold is used today than ever before.
   - Ⓑ Long ago, the Greeks made golden cups.
   - Ⓒ Old paintings show egyptian workers making things of gold.

2. Which sentence has a mistake in punctuation?
   - Ⓐ Gold is soft, but it is also very strong.
   - Ⓑ Gold is used to make rings but it has many other uses.
   - Ⓒ There are gold mines in the United States.

3. Which sentence needs a comma?
   - Ⓐ Gold was found on John Sutter's land in 1848.
   - Ⓑ Sutter lived near Sacramento California.
   - Ⓒ Life in the crowded town and camps was hard.

4. Which sentence has a word that is spelled wrong? Look at the **underlined** words.
   - Ⓐ People have <u>always</u> thought that gold is beautiful.
   - Ⓑ Before long, <u>allmost</u> everyone had heard about the gold.
   - Ⓒ People rushed to California from all <u>across</u> the country.

5. Which sentence has a mistake in grammar?
   - Ⓐ Some gold rings are very old.
   - Ⓑ There is many stories about kings who loved gold.
   - Ⓒ Gold coins were first made about 2,500 years ago.

Answers

1. Ⓐ Ⓑ Ⓒ Ⓓ
2. Ⓐ Ⓑ Ⓒ Ⓓ
3. Ⓐ Ⓑ Ⓒ Ⓓ
4. Ⓐ Ⓑ Ⓒ Ⓓ
5. Ⓐ Ⓑ Ⓒ Ⓓ

How many questions did you get right? Circle your score below. Then fill in your **Mechanics** score on the **Test-Taker Score Chart** on the inside of the back cover.

Number Correct	1	2	3	4	5
Your Score	20	40	60	80	100

Go on ▶

III. Writing

Answer the questions. You may look back at the story as often as you wish.

1. A fact is something that is true. In the box below, list 10 facts about gold.

Facts About Gold

1. _____
2. _____
3. _____
4. _____
5. _____
6. _____
7. _____
8. _____
9. _____
10. _____

2. Write the beginning of a short story called "A Fight Over Gold. Use each of the words in the box in your story.

| friends | found | California | mountain |
| time | digging | wanted | lucky |

A Fight Over Gold

DIRECTIONS
Read this true story about foods from Mexico.
Then answer the questions.

Foods from Mexico

It is a cold winter night. You can hear the wind blowing outside. A cup of hot chocolate would be nice.

When was the last time you had some hot chocolate? Do you know that hot chocolate is a very old drink? It is more than 500 years old.

Chocolate was first made in Mexico. The Native American people who lived in Mexico made it. First, they ground up the beans from the cocoa tree. Next, they added water to the beans to make a drink. They did not put sugar in the drink, so it was not sweet. It was bitter.[1] The word *chocolate* comes from an old Mexican word that means "bitter water."

You may not think of chocolate when you think about Mexican food. You may think of tortillas and burritos. Those are some Mexican foods that many people know. But many other foods first came from Mexico too.

Did you know that corn comes from Mexico? It was grown there more than 5,000 years ago. The early Mexicans loved corn. They used it in many ways. They

1. bitter: not sweet. Something that is bitter has a sharp taste.

For additional exercises and stories about food, see "Clever Grethel" in *Adventures* and "Stone Soup" in *More Adventures* in *Goodman's Five-Star Stories,* Level B.

made flour from corn. They made different kinds of corn soups. They even tossed corn seeds into a fire. Guess what that made? Popcorn!

The tomato came from Mexico too. It was first grown in South America. Later, tomato plants were brought to Mexico. Years later, people brought tomato plants to the United States.

People in the United States are used to eating red tomatoes. But people in Mexico eat both red *and* green tomatoes.

The early Mexicans grew more than just corn and tomatoes. They also grew many kinds of beans and chili (CHILL lee) peppers.

Have you ever tasted chili peppers? If you have, then you know they can be hot! Be careful when you eat them. They can make you feel as if your mouth is on fire.

Some chili peppers are small. Some are long and thin. They can be red, yellow, or green. They can even be black. The early Mexicans loved to add chili peppers to their food. They grew more than 100 different kinds of chili peppers.

Long ago, people ate wild turkeys. They were found all across North America. The early Mexicans were the first to raise turkeys for food.

Today, people in Mexico eat many of the same foods that the early Mexicans ate. They have corn, beans, and chili peppers at many of their meals. They often serve turkey on holidays, just as many families do in the United States.

You may have heard of a Mexican food called the tortilla. A tortilla is a Mexican bread. It is flat and round. It is made from corn flour.

Mexicans often roll up other foods in a tortilla. People may put corn, beans, and chili peppers in a tortilla. They may even add chicken or meat. When food is wrapped in a tortilla, it is called a burrito. It seems that everyone loves burritos. Today, burritos are sold just about everywhere.

As you can see, many different foods came from Mexico. Suppose you went to a movie. You might eat some popcorn. Then you might have a cup of hot chocolate. On the way home, you might stop for a burrito. Well, you can thank the early Mexicans for all these wonderful foods.

I. Reading Skills

Fill in the circle next to the right answer.

1. This story is mostly about
   - Ⓐ ways to use corn.
   - Ⓑ chili peppers.
   - Ⓒ foods that came from Mexico.
   - Ⓓ what people in Mexico eat today.

2. What is chocolate made from?
   - Ⓐ sugar
   - Ⓑ beans
   - Ⓒ candy
   - Ⓓ flour

3. Which sentence is *not* true of chili peppers?
   - Ⓐ They may be red, yellow, or green.
   - Ⓑ They may be hot.
   - Ⓒ Some are small, but many are long and thin.
   - Ⓓ The early Mexicans did not like them.

4. The first tomatoes were grown in
   - Ⓐ South America.
   - Ⓑ North America.
   - Ⓒ China.
   - Ⓓ the United States.

5. What is a tortilla?
   - Ⓐ a flat Mexican bread
   - Ⓑ chili and rice
   - Ⓒ a drink
   - Ⓓ a meal of chicken

6. To make a burrito, you should
   - Ⓐ bake a tortilla.
   - Ⓑ put corn into a fire.
   - Ⓒ roll foods in a tortilla.
   - Ⓓ grind up beans and add water.

Answers

1. Ⓐ Ⓑ Ⓒ Ⓓ
2. Ⓐ Ⓑ Ⓒ Ⓓ
3. Ⓐ Ⓑ Ⓒ Ⓓ
4. Ⓐ Ⓑ Ⓒ Ⓓ
5. Ⓐ Ⓑ Ⓒ Ⓓ
6. Ⓐ Ⓑ Ⓒ Ⓓ

Go on ▶

7. Another good name for this story might be
   Ⓐ Foods That Are Good for You.
   Ⓑ Thank You, Mexico.
   Ⓒ The First Turkeys.
   Ⓓ All About Chili Peppers.

8. They tossed corn seeds into a fire. The word *tossed* means
   Ⓐ threw.
   Ⓑ kicked.
   Ⓒ watched.
   Ⓓ pushed.

9. Many people serve turkey on holidays. As used here, the word *serve* means
   Ⓐ do not like.
   Ⓑ try to find.
   Ⓒ buy in a store.
   Ⓓ put on the table as food.

10. Sometimes food is wrapped in a tortilla. When something is *wrapped,* it is
    Ⓐ lost.
    Ⓑ sold.
    Ⓒ covered on all sides.
    Ⓓ bought in a store.

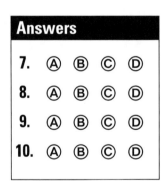

How many questions did you get right? Circle your score below. Then fill in your **Reading Skills** score on the **Test-Taker Score Chart** on the inside of the back cover.

Number Correct	1	2	3	4	5	6	7	8	9	10
My Score	10	20	30	40	50	60	70	80	90	100

Go on ▶

II. Mechanics (capital letters, punctuation, commas, spelling, and grammar)

Fill in the circle next to the right answer.

1. Which sentence needs a capital letter?
   - Ⓐ Wild turkeys were once found all across North America.
   - Ⓑ Many people eat turkey in November at thanksgiving time.
   - Ⓒ The burrito was filled with corn and beans.

2. Which sentence has a mistake in punctuation?
   - Ⓐ These chili peppers are hot!
   - Ⓑ A turkey's egg is bigger than a chicken's egg.
   - Ⓒ I told Luis, "This is a wonderful dinner.

3. Which sentence needs a comma?
   - Ⓐ Corn and chocolate came from Mexico.
   - Ⓑ Do you like popcorn Amy?
   - Ⓒ Some tomatoes are red, but others are green.

4. Which sentence has a word that is spelled wrong? Look at the **underlined** words.
   - Ⓐ The early Mexicans made many diferent kinds of soups.
   - Ⓑ Did you have enough food?
   - Ⓒ Would you like to put some butter on that piece of corn?

5. Which sentence has a mistake in grammar?
   - Ⓐ I visited Mexico. And other countries.
   - Ⓑ My neighbors grow tomatoes in their garden.
   - Ⓒ They also have beans.

Answers

1. Ⓐ Ⓑ Ⓒ Ⓓ
2. Ⓐ Ⓑ Ⓒ Ⓓ
3. Ⓐ Ⓑ Ⓒ Ⓓ
4. Ⓐ Ⓑ Ⓒ Ⓓ
5. Ⓐ Ⓑ Ⓒ Ⓓ

How many questions did you get right? Circle your score below. Then fill in your **Mechanics** score on the **Test-Taker Score Chart** on the inside of the back cover.

Number Correct	1	2	3	4	5
Your Score	20	40	60	80	100

Go on ➤

III. Writing

Answer the questions. You may look back at the story as often as you wish.

1. In each circle below, write a food you like very much.

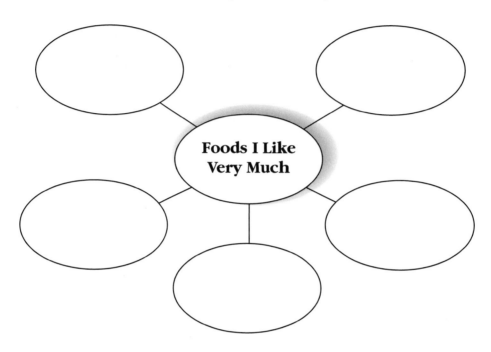

2. Now make up a meal of the foods you like best. Tell about that great meal. What would you have first? What would you have after that? Put as many foods as you wish on each plate.

A Great Meal

_____

_____

_____

_____

_____

_____

Go on ▶

3. Write a letter to a friend. Tell your friend about some foods that came from Mexico.

_____
(Date)

Dear _____,
      (Your friend's name)

_____

_____

_____

_____

_____

_____

_____

_____

_____

Your friend,
(Closing)

_____
(Your name)

DIRECTIONS
Read the story. Then answer the questions.

Li and the Rock

Li was a poor farmer. He lived in a village in China a long time ago. Li worked very hard, but he never managed to save any money.

Li often told his wife, "We will never be rich, but we are happy. That is more important than anything."

One evening Li was walking by the sea. Suddenly, he saw a very large black bird. It was the biggest bird he had ever seen. It had great wide wings.

The bird flew down from the sky. It landed on a pile of earth on the sand.

Li stopped. He said to himself, "That bird is called a koo. I have heard tales about the koo. People say that it rests only on spots where treasure is buried."

For additional exercises and another story set in China, see "The Fight of the Crickets" in *Adventures* in *Goodman's Five-Star Stories,* Level B.

Just then the bird flew away. Li hurried to the pile of earth on the sand. He began to dig into the earth with his hands. Soon his fingers felt something hard. He kept on digging. Then he pulled up a big rock. It was covered with sand.

Li tried to clean the sand off the rock. But the sand was stuck to the rock. It would not come off.

Suddenly Li thought to himself, "Any treasure that is found must be brought to the Emperor.[1] Suppose someone saw the koo land on this spot. Suppose that person saw me digging here. He might tell the Emperor about me. The Emperor could have me killed. I must show this rock to the Emperor."

Li went home to his wife. He told her what happened. Then he said, "I must bring this rock to the Emperor."

"Yes," said Li's wife. "That is what you must do."

The next morning, Li went to the Emperor. Li told the Emperor, "I am a poor farmer. My name is Li. I live in the village of Shen. Last night I was walking by the sea. I saw a koo land on a pile of earth on the sand. I dug into the earth. This is what I found."

Li showed the rock to the Emperor. Then Li said, "I will give this to you as a gift, Emperor."

The Emperor was surprised. He looked closely at the rock. Then he slowly reached out. He held it in his hands. The rock was very heavy. It was dirty and covered with sand.

"What!" said the Emperor. "Do you think this is some treasure? Do you think I am a fool! Are you making fun of me?"

1. **Emperor:** a king.

The Emperor called out angrily, "Take this farmer away! Lock him in a room!"

So they took poor Li away. They put him in a little room and locked the door. Li wondered what to do. But what *could* he do? He took the rock and put it in a corner.

Many months passed. Li's wife did not know where he was. No one sent her word of Li. She was very worried.

Li was in a very cold room. There were holes in the roof. The rainy season came. Every night the rain fell into the room. The rain dropped down on the rock.

One day Li looked at the rock. The rain had washed the sand away. The rock was shiny. It was bright yellow.

Later that day, a man brought Li a bit of food. Li pointed to the rock. He said, "Take me to the Emperor. I must show this to him."

"Come with me," said the man.

Li showed the rock to the Emperor. Li said, "The rain has washed away the sand."

The Emperor was amazed. He said, "This rock is gold! I did not know that when you brought it here. Never have I seen a piece of gold so big!"

Then the Emperor told Li, "You shall have a very fine reward. You will be a rich man. You will never have to work again."

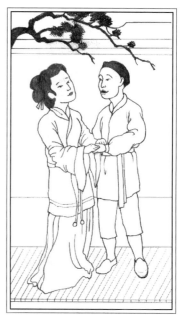

Li bowed and said, "Thank you, Emperor. But most of all I wish to see my wife."

They sent for Li's wife. They brought her to the Emperor's palace.

Li put his arms around his wife. He said to her, "I have something wonderful to tell you."

She said, "I see that you are safe and well. That, alone, is wonderful to me. I was afraid that you were dead."

Li's eyes filled with joy. He smiled as he thought to himself, "How surprised she will be!"

I. Reading Skills

Fill in the circle next to the right answer.

1. This story tells mostly about
   - Ⓐ how a poor farmer became rich.
   - Ⓑ life in China long ago.
   - Ⓒ a bird called a koo.
   - Ⓓ why the Emperor became angry.

2. Which one does *not* belong in Box 1?
   - Ⓐ lived in a village
   - Ⓑ found something in the earth
   - Ⓒ always knew he would be rich
   - Ⓓ lived happily life with his wife

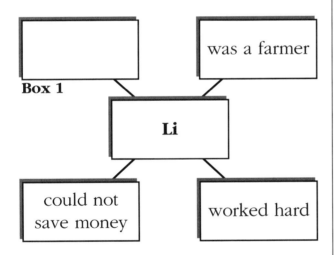

3. At first, no one knew that the rock was gold because
   - Ⓐ the rock did not weigh very much.
   - Ⓑ the rock was covered with sand.
   - Ⓒ the rock was too small to be gold.
   - Ⓓ no one had seen gold before.

4. Which sentence is *not* true?
   - Ⓐ People told the Emperor that Li had been digging in the earth.
   - Ⓑ Li's wife was happy to find that Li was still alive.
   - Ⓒ The koo landed on a spot where there was a treasure.
   - Ⓓ Li was locked in a room for many months.

5. Li's wife was worried about Li because
   - Ⓐ he did not make enough money.
   - Ⓑ he was working too hard.
   - Ⓒ she was afraid that he might lose his job.
   - Ⓓ she did not know what had happened to him.

Answers

1. Ⓐ Ⓑ Ⓒ Ⓓ
2. Ⓐ Ⓑ Ⓒ Ⓓ
3. Ⓐ Ⓑ Ⓒ Ⓓ
4. Ⓐ Ⓑ Ⓒ Ⓓ
5. Ⓐ Ⓑ Ⓒ Ⓓ

6. Li knew that his wife would be surprised when he told her that
   - Ⓐ he had always been poor.
   - Ⓑ he was going to be rich.
   - Ⓒ the Emperor was not going to kill them.
   - Ⓓ he was used to working hard.

7. The story seems to say that
   - Ⓐ a farmer's life is easier than most people think it is.
   - Ⓑ it is good to walk by the sea at night.
   - Ⓒ it is not very hard to find gold.
   - Ⓓ if you do what is right, good things will happen.

8. Li never managed to save any money. The word *managed* means
   - Ⓐ tried.
   - Ⓑ was able.
   - Ⓒ thought about.
   - Ⓓ wanted.

9. He had heard tales about a bird called the koo. The word *tales* means
   - Ⓐ stories.
   - Ⓑ questions.
   - Ⓒ sounds.
   - Ⓓ surprises.

10. The Emperor said that Li would get a reward. As used here, the word *reward* means
    - Ⓐ help.
    - Ⓑ a house with a garden.
    - Ⓒ money given for doing a good thing.
    - Ⓓ a ride home.

Answers

6.	Ⓐ	Ⓑ	Ⓒ	Ⓓ
7.	Ⓐ	Ⓑ	Ⓒ	Ⓓ
8.	Ⓐ	Ⓑ	Ⓒ	Ⓓ
9.	Ⓐ	Ⓑ	Ⓒ	Ⓓ
10.	Ⓐ	Ⓑ	Ⓒ	Ⓓ

How many questions did you get right? Circle your score below. Then fill in your **Reading Skills** score on the **Test-Taker Score Chart** on the inside of the back cover.

Number Correct	1	2	3	4	5	6	7	8	9	10
My Score	10	20	30	40	50	60	70	80	90	100

Go on ▶

II. Mechanics (capital letters, punctuation, the comma, spelling, and grammar)

Fill in the circle next to the right answer.

1. Which sentence needs a capital letter?
   - Ⓐ The name of this story is "Li and the rock."
   - Ⓑ The bird rested on a pile of earth near the sea.
   - Ⓒ They lived in China a long time ago.

2. Which sentence has a mistake in punctuation?
   - Ⓐ The sand wouldn't come off the rock.
   - Ⓑ Li's room wasn't warm.
   - Ⓒ She didnt know where Li was.

3. Which sentence needs a comma?
   - Ⓐ The bird flew into the air and Li hurried to the place where it had been.
   - Ⓑ The rock was dirty, heavy, and covered with sand.
   - Ⓒ Li gave the golden rock to the Emperor, and the Emperor was pleased.

4. Which sentence has a word that is spelled wrong? Look at the **underlined** words.
   - Ⓐ The Emperor was <u>too</u> angry to talk to Li.
   - Ⓑ Li did not know the rock was gold <u>untill</u> the rain washed away the sand.
   - Ⓒ When the Emperor saw that the rock was gold, he could not <u>believe</u> his eyes.

5. Which sentence has a mistake in grammar?
   - Ⓐ Li took the rock home.
   - Ⓑ Li went to see the Emperor.
   - Ⓒ Li's wife thought that Li done the right thing.

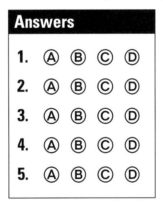

Answers
1. Ⓐ Ⓑ Ⓒ Ⓓ
2. Ⓐ Ⓑ Ⓒ Ⓓ
3. Ⓐ Ⓑ Ⓒ Ⓓ
4. Ⓐ Ⓑ Ⓒ Ⓓ
5. Ⓐ Ⓑ Ⓒ Ⓓ

How many questions did you get right? Circle your score below. Then fill in your **Mechanics** score on the **Test-Taker Score Chart** on the inside of the back cover.

Number Correct	1	2	3	4	5
Your Score	20	40	60	80	100

Go on ▶

III. Writing

Answer the questions. You may look back at the story as often as you wish.

1. Why did Li bring the rock to the Emperor?

   _____
   _____
   _____
   _____

2. Why did the Emperor tell his men to lock Li in a room?

   _____
   _____
   _____
   _____

3. Do you think the Emperor should have told Li's wife that Li was locked in a room? Explain your answer.

   _____
   _____
   _____
   _____
   _____

4. The Emperor was going to make Li a rich man. Explain why.

_____
_____
_____
_____
_____
_____
_____

5. Do you think Li loved gold more than he loved his wife? Do you think Li's wife loved gold more than she loved Li? Explain your answers.

_____
_____
_____
_____
_____
_____
_____
_____

DIRECTIONS
Read this true story about wolves. Then answer the questions.

All About the Wolf

It can smell an animal more than one mile away. It can hear another animal more than three miles away. It can run through the snow for 25 miles without resting. It can even go for many days without eating.

What animal is this? It is the wolf.

A wolf has a bushy tale and looks like a large dog. Like dogs, wolves are covered with hair called fur. A wolf's fur is thicker than a dog's fur. This thick fur keeps the wolf warm when it is very cold outside.

You can see wolves in a zoo, of course. But most wolves live in the wild. Gray wolves like places that have a lot of snow. That is why Canada has about 40,000 gray wolves. Some wolves even live near the North Pole.

Most wolves are gray. Some wolves are red or black. The wolves that live near the North Pole are white.

Some wolves weigh as much as 175 pounds. A very large wolf can be more than six feet long from its nose to the end of its tail. But most wolves are not big at all. They do not weigh more than about 40 pounds.

For additional exercises and a story in which a wolf plays an important role, see "The Tale of the Wolf" in *More Adventures* in *Goodman's Five-Star Stories*, Level B.

Many people think that wolves live alone. This is not true. Wolves live in groups. The groups are called packs. Most packs have from 5 to 12 wolves.

Wolf packs are like families. The older wolves take care of the baby wolves, which are called pups. When the pups grow up, they start their own packs.

The strongest wolves lead the pack. They tell the other wolves where to go and what to do. They tell them what to hunt. When a wolf pack travels, the strongest wolves are always in front.

The wolf pack must work together to stay alive. Most of the time wolves hunt large animals like deer and moose. But wolves also hunt small animals like rabbits and mice.

Wolves are very good hunters. This is because they can hear and smell very well. A wolf's hearing is so good that it can hear a mouse moving under the snow.

Sometimes a pack will hunt an animal for many hours. The pack may even follow the animal for days. Then all the wolves in the pack unite to attack and kill the animal.

After the kill, the wolves eat as much as they can. Each wolf eats from 10 to 20 pounds of meat. The wolves may bury pieces of meat in the ground. Then they come back later to eat the meat.

Wolves do more than just hunt. They are not always fierce. Wolves love to play. They run, jump, and chase each other.

It is easy to tell how a wolf feels. The wolf's face tells how it feels. When a wolf is happy, its mouth is open. Its tongue hangs out. When a wolf is angry, it shows its teeth.

Like a dog, a wolf also barks. But wolves are best known for their long, loud howl.[1] Why do wolves howl? They howl to one another in the morning to say hello. They howl to find one another. Wolves howl when they need help. They also howl to warn other wolves about trouble.

Many people are very frightened by wolves. People may feel this way because wolves in fables and fairy tales attack people. In real life, a wolf almost never attacks a person. Wolves are afraid of people. When a wolf sees a person, it runs away.

Wolves avoid people, but people do not stay away from wolves. People move on to land where wolves live. That land is now covered with ranches and farms. There is less and less space where wolves can live. More important, there are fewer wild animals for the wolf to hunt.

People also kill many wolves. People fear that hungry wolves might eat their farm animals.

Today, wolves are beginning to be seen in more places. Not long ago, there were no wolves in Yellowstone National Park. All the wolves had been killed. Now park workers are bringing wolves back to the park.

Maybe one day you will go to Yellowstone Park in Wyoming. Late at night, you might hear loud howls. Do not be afraid. It is only some wolves. They are having a good talk!

1. **howl:** to give a long, loud cry.

I. Reading Skills

Fill in the circle next to the right answer.

1. Another good name for this story might be
   - Ⓐ The Wolf: A Very Surprising Animal.
   - Ⓑ Why Wolves Are Good Hunters.
   - Ⓒ How Much Wolves Weigh
   - Ⓓ Wolves in Yellowstone National Park.

2. Wolves can live in very cold places because they
   - Ⓐ are large, heavy animals.
   - Ⓑ can always find caves to stay in.
   - Ⓒ have very thick fur.
   - Ⓓ are very strong.

3. Which sentence is true?
   - Ⓐ Wolves cannot hear very well.
   - Ⓑ Most wolves are white.
   - Ⓒ Wolves like places where there is a lot of snow.
   - Ⓓ Most wolves live alone.

4. When a wolf shows its teeth, it means that the wolf is
   - Ⓐ happy.
   - Ⓑ angry.
   - Ⓒ tired.
   - Ⓓ sad.

5. The story says that if a wolf sees a person, it will probably
   - Ⓐ move closer to the person.
   - Ⓑ bite the person.
   - Ⓒ try to become friendly with the person.
   - Ⓓ stay away from the person.

6. The writer seems to feel that wolves
   - Ⓐ are bad animals that should be killed.
   - Ⓑ should be kept as pets.
   - Ⓒ are never harmed by people.
   - Ⓓ are smarter and less frightening than most people think they are.

Answers

1. Ⓐ Ⓑ Ⓒ Ⓓ
2. Ⓐ Ⓑ Ⓒ Ⓓ
3. Ⓐ Ⓑ Ⓒ Ⓓ
4. Ⓐ Ⓑ Ⓒ Ⓓ
5. Ⓐ Ⓑ Ⓒ Ⓓ
6. Ⓐ Ⓑ Ⓒ Ⓓ

Go on ▶

7. It is fair to say that wolves
   - Ⓐ work and play together.
   - Ⓑ almost never help each other.
   - Ⓒ cannot go for more than a day without food.
   - Ⓓ get tired very quickly.

8. Wolves unite to attack and kill other animals. The word *unite* means
   - Ⓐ run away from.
   - Ⓑ play with.
   - Ⓒ join together.
   - Ⓓ take care of.

9. Wolves do not hunt all the time, and they are not always fierce. The word *fierce* means
   - Ⓐ wild.
   - Ⓑ friendly.
   - Ⓒ angry.
   - Ⓓ hungry.

10. The story says that wolves avoid people. The word *avoid* means
    - Ⓐ know about.
    - Ⓑ keep away from.
    - Ⓒ forget about.
    - Ⓓ think about.

Answers

7. Ⓐ Ⓑ Ⓒ Ⓓ
8. Ⓐ Ⓑ Ⓒ Ⓓ
9. Ⓐ Ⓑ Ⓒ Ⓓ
10. Ⓐ Ⓑ Ⓒ Ⓓ

How many questions did you get right? Circle your score below. Then fill in your **Reading Skills** score on the **Test-Taker Score Chart** on the inside of the back cover.

Number Correct	1	2	3	4	5	6	7	8	9	10
My Score	10	20	30	40	50	60	70	80	90	100

Go on ▶

II. Mechanics (capital letters, punctuation, the comma, spelling, and grammar)

Fill in the circle next to the right answer.

1. Which sentence needs a capital letter?
   - Ⓐ Ranches and farms cover land where wolves used to live.
   - Ⓑ There are some wolves that live near the North Pole.
   - Ⓒ Have you ever visited yellowstone Park in Wyoming?

2. Which sentence is not punctuated correctly?
   - Ⓐ Mr and Mrs Akimo sometimes see wolves on their land.
   - Ⓑ Dogs like to bark, but wolves like to howl.
   - Ⓒ Dr. C. W. Sanchez has studied the lives of wolves.

3. Which sentence needs a comma?
   - Ⓐ Jack London, a great writer, wrote stories about wolves.
   - Ⓑ Have you ever read any of Jack London's stories Ada?
   - Ⓒ Yes, I have read some of his stories.

4. Which sentence has a word that is spelled wrong? Look at the **underlined** words.
   - Ⓐ Sometimes a wolf shows its teeth.
   - Ⓑ Wolves can hunt very well because there hearing is so good.
   - Ⓒ The strongest wolf tries to help the other wolves.

5. Which one has a mistake in grammar?
   - Ⓐ I liked this story, it was interesting.
   - Ⓑ The other stories were also interesting.
   - Ⓒ They are fun to read.

Answers

1. Ⓐ Ⓑ Ⓒ Ⓓ
2. Ⓐ Ⓑ Ⓒ Ⓓ
3. Ⓐ Ⓑ Ⓒ Ⓓ
4. Ⓐ Ⓑ Ⓒ Ⓓ
5. Ⓐ Ⓑ Ⓒ Ⓓ

How many questions did you get right? Circle your score below. Then fill in your **Mechanics** score on the **Test-Taker Score Chart** on the inside of the back cover.

Number Correct	1	2	3	4	5
Your Score	20	40	60	80	100

Go on ➤

III. Writing

Answer the questions. You may look back at the story as often as you wish.

1. This story gives many facts (things that are true) about wolves. In the box below, write the five facts about wolves that you found the most interesting.

5 Interesting Facts About Wolves

1.

2.

3.

4.

5.

2. Explain why wolves howl.

_____

_____

_____

_____

_____

_____

_____

Go on ▶

3. Why are there fewer wolves today than there were years ago?

___

4. Did this story change the way you feel about wolves? Explain your answer.

___

All About the Wolf 63